Me and My Fri

A play

Gillian Plowman

Samuel French – London

New York – Sydney – Toronto – Hollywood

ME AND MY FRIEND

First produced at the Soho Poly, London on 12th April
1990, with the following cast:

Bunny	Steve Swinscoe
Oz	Tim Stern
Robin	Sonia Ritter
Julia	Nicola Redmond

Directed by Deborah Paige
Designed by Lucy Weller
Lighting by Tina MacHugh
Sound by John Leonard

CHARACTERS

Bunny }
Oz } The two men

Robin }
Julia } The two women

Act I   The men's flat
Act II   The women's flat
Act III   The men's flat

The flats are council property used for the rehabilitation of patients released from psychiatric hospital

Time—the present

NB. The first two acts may be presented individually as one-act plays, but the third act may not.

ACT I

The men's flat

Bunny and Oz live together in this flat. There is a bed on either side of the room and a large table in the centre. There is an ironing board, iron, clothes, etc. about the place. There are doors to the kitchen and the hall. The telephone is an important feature

Bunny stands in his underclothes, ironing a suit. Oz is clearing the table in order to make it look like an office. Then they both dress in suits that are not quite modern and smart. Oz sits at the table

Bunny goes off to the kitchen and knocks to come in. He then quickly comes into the room to be Oz's secretary

Bunny (*as the secretary; to Oz*) Mr Marshall to see you, sir. (*To himself*) Mr Burkwood will see you now, sir.

Bunny comes and stands in front of the "desk". Oz eyes him up and down. Bunny extends his hand

Good-morning, Mr Burkwood. (*Pause*) He'd say it first.
Oz He might not. (*Oz ignores the outstretched hand*)
Bunny Shall I sit down?
Oz Please sit down, Mr Marshall.

There is no chair. Bunny stops, looks unhappy

Bunny I . . . farted.
Oz You don't have to tell him that.
Bunny He'll know.
Oz He'll ignore it.
Bunny I always do when I'm nervous. The chair wasn't ready. (*He fetches it from under the ironing, places it and sits*)
Oz Excuse me a moment, Mr Marshall. (*He gets a spray and sprays the room*)
Bunny Sorry, Mr Burkwood. That's not air freshener.
Oz What?
Bunny Hair lacquer. You bought it.
Oz It's best if you just answer questions, Mr Marshall.

Silence. He combs and sprays the back of Bunny's head

Appearances are awfully important.
Bunny Oh yes, Mr Burkwood.
Oz No, that was me.

Bunny You.
Oz Yes.
Bunny Oz.
Oz Yes.
Bunny Oz?
Oz Yes?
Bunny You know about the hole, don't you?
Oz Where? (*He checks his suit*)
Bunny In the ozone layer.

Oz checks under his arms

In Antarctica. There's a big hole.
Oz In the ice?
Bunny In the ozone layer. It's letting in radiation. It could kill us, Oz.
Oz We're not in Antarctica.
Bunny You've squirted three times.
Oz Have I?
Bunny Chlorofluorocarbons.
Oz You did it, not me.
Bunny Every time you squirt the aerosol tin, it makes the hole bigger.
Oz In Antarctica.
Bunny It spreads there.
Oz As long as it stays there, we're all right, aren't we?
Bunny The radiation will come through the hole and go all over the place, and we'll get skin cancer.
Oz Oh shit, oh shit. As if we haven't got enough problems. They told us, Bun, not to worry about the things we can't do anything about. Just concentrate on the little day-by-day things, or everything will get out of proportion. We've got unemployment to worry about. People finding holes in the ozone layer are scientists, and then reporters report it and newspaper editors print it, and they're all employed, so they haven't got that to worry about, have they. Why do you have to read about these things, Bun?
Bunny We can do something about it.
Oz What?
Bunny Stop squirting chlorofluorocarbons. Everybody must stop squirting them. Stop buying them. Stop making them.
Oz More people out of work.
Bunny You can make things without chlorofluorocarbons.
Oz You just like saying it.
Bunny Yes I do. I like long intelligent words. I like long intelligent conversations. Mendacious, lugubrious, ubiquitous—I want to use them. I'm sick to death of the fuddlement in people's heads. Including mine. Do you know, there was a time when the longest word I could think of was weasel. Nobody could talk about weasels. Talk about weasels, Oz. Go on.
Oz Old-fashioned sailors used to get them in their biscuits.
Bunny That's weevils. I don't know why I agreed to live with you. You don't know anything.

Oz I know about the hole, actually.

Bunny Do you?

Oz Oh yes.

Bunny And you'll stop squirting things?

Oz There'll be no squirting in this office, Mr Marshall. Excuse me. My secretary seems to have left the iron on.

Bunny Oh.

Oz goes and switches it off

Oz She's a fine girl. A fine secretary. She's young and blonde. She'll do anything for me, you know.

Bunny Good staff is very important, Mr Burkwood.

Oz You can call me Brian.

Bunny I don't know what his name is. (*He gets out a piece of paper*) A. Burkwood.

Oz A burk would! (*He laughs*) Aubrey.

Bunny I don't know.

Oz Yes. Aubrey. References?

Bunny Oh yes, I've got references. Here. Be careful with them ...

Oz Aubrey.

Bunny Are you sure?

Oz He might do, mightn't he? If you're going to be working together.

Bunny They're real, Oz.

Oz Mr Burkwood!

Bunny You're making me nervous.

Oz passes him the hair lacquer

No squirting!

Oz Use an umbrella! That'll catch it! It won't get to Antarctica. And he might want to call you by your Christian name. Well, he will.

Pause

Bunny Bunny. I was christened Bunny.

Oz waits for an explanation

Oz My mother wouldn't have done that to me.

Bunny My mother didn't. She wanted Bernard proper so she could call me Bunny for short. My father got it the wrong way round when he went to the registrar's. He was a very nervous man, too.

Oz The registrar?

Bunny My father was. And the registrar. He worried about getting people's names right. He told my father, and my father told me, and I've remembered it ever since, which is especially useful in my work, well anybody's, that a person's name is his most personal thing, and it's most important to get it perfectly correct, otherwise it upsets them. You would be if I called you Iz, or Az or Uz, wouldn't you?

Pause

Oz So your mother called you Bernard for short.

Bunny Only when I was little. She called me by my proper name after I started school.

Oz And your father?

Bunny She called him by his proper name. Names are very important.

Oz Right, then ... Bunny. Do you have your c.v.?

Bunny My curriculum vitae? Yes.

Oz I know what it means. (*He reads it*) I assume you wouldn't make passes at my secretary?

Bunny Oh no ... Aubrey.

Oz I expect you like blondes.

Bunny My wife had red hair.

Oz With big chests and round bottoms and white teeth and lipstick and nail varnish. Don't you?

Bunny Yes, I do, Mr Burkwood, but ...

Oz You leave my secretary alone, or you're fired. Got that?

Bunny Yes.

Pause

Oz What experience have you had?

Bunny Lots.

Oz Tell me.

Bunny It's down there.

Oz I don't want to read it. Tell me about it.

Bunny I got four O levels. Those. (*He points*) I was apprenticed to a printing firm and stayed with them for ten years. Printing things.

Oz looks enquiringly

Posters, leaflets, brochures, magazines ... really interesting work.

Oz Magazines. With women in?

Bunny No.

Oz No.

Bunny No.

Oz I don't like red-haired women.

Bunny No.

Oz Then what?

Bunny I took evening classes in management and business studies. ONC. There. (*He points*) And applied for a job as a print manager. Rival firm, but it has to be done, doesn't it? Short-listed six out of fifteen applicants, and I got it! Print Manager! A big section. Eight men. They all looked to me. I looked after them. Oh yes. They really respected me because I worked hard. I hardly ever went home. Too much work to do. Manager's job, you see. No-one else could do it. Committed, the boss said. The Managing Director. Mr Smithers. He's written one of the references. He respected me. You see—conscientious, reliable, always on the spot ...

Oz There's a gap.

Bunny What?

Oz You left that job two years ago.

Bunny You said you didn't want to read it.

Oz I changed my mind. He's allowed to do that.

Bunny I felt the time had come for a change, Mr Burkwood.

Pause

Oz Well?

Bunny So I went abroad.

Oz To work?

Bunny Oh yes.

Oz Where did you go?

Bunny To Israel. To work on a kibbutz. For the experience.

Oz And what did you do?

Bunny Kibbutzi things ...

Oz Mr Marshall, you're not a Jew, are you?

Bunny No! I was born in Edinburgh. It could have been Australia, just as easily.

Oz How could your mother have got from Edinburgh to Australia in time?

Bunny Where I went to work. I thought Israel would be more interesting. More than Australia ... I can't bloody tell them where I was, Oz, can I? Nobody wants to know if you've been there. You'll never get a job if they know that.

Oz I'm sorry. You haven't got the job.

Bunny There you are. I told you!

Oz All this travelling isn't relevant.

Bunny I haven't been travelling!

Oz Your time's up. Next please.

Bunny I've been a manager. You only want a sales assistant in a bicycle shop. I'm lowering myself.

Oz Lowering yourself? Lowering yourself? My sales assistants are on a pinnacle.

Bunny I can work on a pinnacle ...

Oz Thank you, Mr Marshall. Caroline, see Mr Marshall out ...

Bunny I'm smart and presentable and I can add up ...

Oz If he's finished with you, he's finished with you ...

Bunny gets angry

Bunny I'm very good with people. They respect me.

Oz Thank you, Mr Marshall.

Bunny And I believe the fucking customer is always right. (*He grabs Oz by the collar*)

Oz All right—you've got the job.

Bunny lets go

Bunny Thank you very much, Mr Burkwood. When would you like me to start?

Oz Caroline, get me a cup of tea, would you. And show Mr Marshall out.

Bunny Certainly, darling Mr Burkwood. This way, darling Mr Marshall. I'm so glad you're going to join us.

He sees himself out, then reappears diffidently

Oz It won't do, Bunny.

Bunny No?

Oz You lost your temper.

Bunny I got the job.

Oz No you didn't. He was under duress. He changed his mind.

Bunny I don't want to work for him anyway. He's obviously schizophrenic.

Oz How many interviews have you got?

Bunny I hate his secretary. She's got a patronizing ...

Oz Bottom.

Bunny And superior ...

Oz Tits.

Bunny And she altogether reeks of ...

Oz Come and get it, Ozzie.

Bunny You know your trouble, don't you?

Oz Yes. Do you want to practise another interview?

Bunny No. You don't do it properly.

They take off their suits

I saw a woman on the stairs today. Going up.

Oz And?

Bunny There's a woman upstairs, that's all.

Oz I know that. I knew that before you did. I saw her on the stairs ages ago. Last week. I saw her first.

Bunny Did she speak to you?

Oz No.

Bunny She spoke to me.

Oz Stop! I don't want to talk about it any more.

Bunny What?

Oz Sex.

Bunny All right.

Pause

Oz ... ?

Oz Done! Finished! Done!

Pause

Bunny It was the only one.

Oz The only what? Woman going upstairs?

Bunny Job interview I've got.

Oz Then you'd better go for it. That's what they told us to do. That's why we have to practise. Go for all the interviews you can. It's good experience.

Bunny I don't like him.

Oz It was me, Bunny.

Bunny I don't like you.

Oz You blow hot and cold, you do.

Bunny At least I am trying to get a job. You haven't applied for anything yet.

Oz I'm doing the flat, aren't I? Somebody's got to do the flat. The cleaning ... (*he tidies up*) ... the shopping ...

Bunny We do it together.

Oz Not when you're out at work, you won't, will you. You won't do it then. The cooking ... here's a pie and here's a tart ...

He brings them in

I do it because there are no women. I should be living with a woman, Bunny, 'cos that's what they do. Pies and tarts. THEN I'd go and find myself a job.

Bunny (*singing*) Which came first, the woman or the job? The job or the woman, or the woman or the job?

Oz They should have let us practise that as well. Living with women. That would have been good experience.

Oz goes off to the kitchen and brings in a tray with cutlery, potatoes and bread

Potatoes. Bread. Garlic bread.

Bunny puts on a dressing-gown, and walks on his toes, as though in high heels

Bunny I'm a woman.

Oz What?

Bunny I'm incredibly attractive, and we've just met. Go on, say something.

Oz You're incredibly attractive.

Bunny Why, thank you.

Oz Would you like some potatoes?

Bunny Not really. We've only just met.

Oz So?

Bunny I thought you said potatoes.

Oz I did say potatoes.

Bunny But you meant ...

Oz I meant potatoes.

Bunny Not "per-tay-tows"? (*He juggles with his hands suggestively*)

Oz What if I had?

Bunny I'm not that kind of girl.

Oz How do I know what kind of girl you are.

Bunny By looking at me.

Oz looks at him

Oz Shit, Bunny, I can't tell what kind of girl you are. I never could. I took a girl fishing once who got sea-sick and didn't like maggots. And I took a girl to the cinema who couldn't see anything but wouldn't wear glasses. I told her I liked women who wore glasses, and she put them on, and wanted to watch the film. I asked this very nice girl to tea to meet my mother, and she didn't show up.

Bunny I expect your mother was disappointed.

Oz My mother didn't show up.

Bunny (*as the girl*) All this tea and no mother.

Oz Mummy! That's what she likes to be called.

Bunny Mummy!

Oz But only by me.

Bunny Sorry.

An awkward pause

Oz Would you like to sit down.

Bunny Thank you. You have a very nice house.

Oz I help her keep it nice. What time is it?

Bunny Four o'clock.

Oz Gone to fetch a last-minute something or other. She shouldn't have done. We got everything. We made a list and we went to the supermarket. She was going to talk to you.

Bunny sidles up to Oz

Bunny You talk to me.

Oz What about?

Bunny Dogs?

Oz Barky things.

Bunny They are, aren't they?

Oz Unless muzzled.

Bunny How astute you are.

Oz Furry things.

Bunny I like furry things.

Oz Do you?

Bunny Kittens, and coats and chests ...

Oz pushes Bunny away

Oz She'll be here soon.

Bunny sits and picks at the food

Don't.

Bunny Sorry. Would you like me to put the kettle on?

Oz No! Mummy wouldn't like that. She never came. She walked into the road and hit a silver-grey Ford Granada two point eight. She left me on my own in that house to talk to that girl.

Bunny (*as himself*) She probably meant to return.

Oz No she didn't. She died. She was really stupid, Bunny, dying like that. She didn't get me up in the mornings any more. Do you know how early postmen have to get up? Four o'clock. I was born at four o'clock in the morning. Mummy always said I should be a postman. But I couldn't get up any more and I got the letters all wrong and they didn't trust me any more. Do you know what they said? "You can keep your hat."

Bunny You wore the hat all the time at the hospital.

Oz Yes, I did.

Bunny I thought you were very funny.

Oz Yes.

Bunny You made me laugh. Called me the man in Five-B.

Oz Good-morning, man in Five-B.

Bunny Good-morning, postman. Any mail?

Oz We're all male!

They laugh

I don't know what else to be, Bun. I'm not qualified like you.

Bunny You could be a chef. Your pastry's very good.

Oz Yes! In a restaurant where they have beautiful waitresses in tight black dresses with frilly . . .

Bunny Newspaper! Look for chef jobs.

They both kneel on the floor, looking in the local paper

Have you been circumcised?

Oz Do you have to be, to be a chef? I didn't have to be, to be a postman.

Bunny It's just that I've noticed there's often drips around the toilet where you've missed.

Oz That's not me.

Bunny There's no-one else uses our toilet.

Oz You.

Bunny I've been circumcised.

Oz So?

Bunny It goes straight. Here's one. Baker's Oven. Must be experienced.

Oz Does it hurt?

Bunny Here's the number to ring.

Oz I liked delivering parcels most of all. Seeing the look on people's faces when you knock on the door and you've got a parcel for them. I wish I could do that again.

Bunny Write to the Post Office then.

Oz They don't want me back.

Bunny Then ring the Baker's Oven.

Oz It's my confidence, you see. I've lost a bit of it.

Bunny I know that.

Oz Haven't quite got it back.

Bunny Being circumcised gives you more confidence.

Oz How?

Bunny 'Cos you know everything's in order. Neat and tidy. Ship-shape. Bristol fashion. You know you won't get any wet patches on your trousers just before an interview. Confidence.

Pause

Oz Bunny?

Bunny What?

Oz Could I have a look?

Bunny No! If you were back there, you'd be on bread and water for a week for saying that.

Oz We're not though, are we? There's nobody spying on us anymore. We can do what we like.

Bunny Well, I'm not showing you.
Oz Well, I'm not getting circumcised.
Bunny Well, I'm not cleaning up your drips.
Oz Pretend we're rugby players.
Bunny Why?
Oz The whole team jumps in the shower with no clothes on.
Bunny Two people aren't exactly a team.
Oz I can be a team! Be a team, Bun. Scrum down.

They do a scrum, heaving and groaning, then run around each other throwing a rolled-up shirt for a ball. Oz whistles

Oz We won! We won! Into the showers.

They jump into an imaginary shower and "splash" each other. They sing

Both (*singing*) "If I were the marrying kind, which thank the Lord I'm not, sir, the kind of girl that I would wed would be a rugby scrum half . . ."

Bunny pulls out his shorts by the elastic. Oz looks down

Oz Oh yes, I see.
Both (*singing*) "I'd push hard, she'd push hard, we'd both push hard together . . ."
Oz Where's that number?

Bunny sings, Oz rings

Bunny (*singing*) "We'll be all right in the middle of the night, pushing hard together . . ."
Oz Hallo, I'd like to enquire about a circumcision.

Silence. He puts the phone down. Bunny takes the number out of his hand

Bunny (*quietly*) That's the Baker's Oven.

Oz is devastated

Oz What must they think of me?
Bunny They won't know who you are.
Oz They told me to try the butcher's.
Bunny It was a mistake.
Oz You gave me the wrong number. You don't want me to go out to work. You want me to stay here, and cook tarts, and pee straight.
Bunny They won't know it's you. Write and apply.
Oz They'll recognize my voice.
Bunny Not in a letter.
Oz When I get there.
Bunny It doesn't sound the same voice when you get there as it does on the phone.
Oz The only chance I had and you had to go and spoil it for me.
Bunny I was only trying to help.
Oz I don't need that sort of help.

Bunny Do it yourself then. You're the one who keeps moaning about unemployment, and having nothing to do but kick around here all day . . .

Oz Working my fingers to the bone . . .

Bunny But you don't do anything about it.

Oz I want to! I phoned them up. You gave me the wrong number.

Bunny I gave you the right number.

Oz See if there's something else.

Bunny You see if there's something else. You're old enough and bloody ugly enough.

Oz I know I'm ugly. I'm fat and ugly and you don't care about me . . .

Bunny's wife's words come back to him

Bunny You work all day and nearly all night in that bloody factory and you never think of me, waiting at home, looking after the kids, trying to keep meals hot for someone who can't even be bothered to say thank you, when he does manage to get home, and then falls fast asleep. I might just as well be a lump of lard. I need someone to talk to, Bunny. That's what husbands are for. To talk to you, and give you a hug when you've had a busy day, and play with the kids, and love you in bed. But you can't do that, can you? Too tired to raise your little finger, let alone . . . Stop it, Mary, stop it! I ache. Everything hurts. I can't love you and work—it hurts, it hurts, it hurts . . . Go away, Mary. She was always on my fucking back, Mary.

Oz I didn't like Mary. When she came to visit you. She wouldn't talk to me. I was pleased when she said she wasn't coming any more.

Pause

Bunny You can't have work and women, Oz. You can't. You have to choose.

Oz I'm glad you got a divorce, Bunny. She was a horrible woman. She wouldn't even look at me.

Bunny She didn't like your hat.

Oz gets his postman's hat and puts it on. Bunny laughs

Oz I'm going to make a parcel. I haven't made a parcel for ages. (*He has a special parcel-making kit*)

Bunny The last one you made was for me.

Oz You couldn't guess, could you?

Bunny It was in a box. I couldn't see the shape.

Oz And it was well-packed and padded, so you couldn't hear it.

Bunny But I bought it.

Oz But I parcelled it.

Bunny And I opened it.

Oz And I used it. (*He goes to look at the telephone*) And now I've used it again, and I did it all wrong.

Bunny I'll find you another number.

Oz I'm so stupid.

Bunny I was stupid.

Oz Were you?

Bunny Yes.

Oz Are you sure? With all that reading you do?

Bunny What are you going to put in this parcel?

Oz A dress. I've got some dresses. My mother's. She left them when she hit
    the Granada. (*He gets a suitcase and turfs out his own clothes until he finds
    some white tissue paper. He takes this out carefully, and from underneath
    that, some carefully folded dresses*) Which one, Bun?

Bunny The red one.

Oz The red one, right. Wrap it in tissue paper. (*He does this*) Then in nice
    brown parcel paper. Hold the sellotape, Bun. (*He sings to the tune of "I
    Do Like To Be Beside the Seaside"*) "Oh I do like to make a little parcel
    ..."

Bunny You've got all the gear, haven't you?

Oz Parcel-making gear, oh yes. String, scissors. Right, pass the sellotape.
    (*He sticks some on. He continues to the tune of "I Do Like To Be Beside the
    Seaside"*) "A parcel is such a lovely thing" ... Pass the parcel, Bun. Pass
    the parcel!

> I do like to make a little parcel
> With brown paper and string

They la la, passing the parcel to and fro till they stop the "music"

Bunny Open it. Open it.

Oz No. (*He ties string on it*) It's not for us.

Bunny Who's it for then?

Oz (*writing*) The lady in number seventeen ...

Bunny The lady in number seventeen?

Oz Elm Court, Copnor.

Bunny Who's that?

Oz nods upward

    Oh.

Oz Stamp. (*He sticks one on*) Postmark. London. North West eight. (*He
    has a little stamping kit and stamps the parcel*) Bloody good, isn't it?

Bunny Bloody good, yes.

Oz Right. (*He gets a mail bag out of the suitcase*)

Bunny Shouldn't you have given that back?

Oz Crafty me. I had two. Only gave one back. I'm off to work. Off on my
    rounds. Got a lot to do today. One of the other postmen is off sick. See
    you when I get back then. Toodle-oo.

Bunny Oz! Don't go to work without me. Oz!

Oz exits with the parcel

Bunny finds his letter and reads

    "Dear Mr Marshall, Thank you for your interest in the above vacancy. I
    should be pleased if you would attend for an interview on ..." Mr
    Burkwood, I do want to work for you. If it could just be from nine till

half-past five. I'd come in before nine, of course to get everything ready, all neat and tidy and ship-shape and Bristol fashion. And I'll smile at the customers, and I won't mind working through the lunch hour if that will save you shutting, and of course, I know the shop might close at five thirty, but there are all sorts of things to do after that, like balancing the money in the till ... well, things ... but I have to get home if that's all right. Mary didn't like being left on her own all the time—my wife—and I don't want to make the same mistake again. Well, Oz isn't my wife, but I want to get it right. No I have to go home—he'll be alone. No, he's gone to work. It's only pretend. He's not really a postman. He was. Mr Burkwood, you've got to give me a job. I can't be here on my own. Not on my own. I'll get ready. Wash. Have a shave ... (*He puts shaving foam on his face, then tries to take off his tie*) Have I got a clean shirt? (*He puts a shirt on the ironing board, then checks his chin. He decides to change his razor blade*) Mr Burkwood, you see, appearances are important—I don't need to tell you that. And smell, yes. Oh God, I farted. (*He squirts the hair lacquer, then finds the umbrella and puts it up*) It's only when I'm nervous ... you've got to know you look good from the top of your head to the heel of your shoe. Gives you confidence. And I have been circumcised. (*He is now in a mess and goes to iron his shirt*) Oz! You switched the sodding iron off. I wouldn't swear in front of the customers, Mr Burkwood. Can I help you, madam? Ah, Mr Brown, how good of you to call again. It's no good having creases in your shirt. Or bad breath. I know that. (*He squirts some hair lacquer into his mouth and drops the razor. He looks about him, and slowly sinks to the ground. He breaks down*) I'm scared, Mr Burkwood. I'm scared of having a job, and I'm scared of not having a job. (*He picks up the razor blade and cuts his wrists*)

There is a whistling and Oz returns

Oz I'm back. I've had a hard day, you know. Gosh, I could eat a horse. (*He steps over all the mess, sits down and starts to eat*) Why are you sitting on the floor, Bun?

Bunny I'm tired.

Oz It's wonderful being back at work, you know. I've got a very nice round. Not the same as before, but variety is the spice of life, don't they say.

Bunny You're not back at work.

Oz I took the parcel up, Bun. There was no reply. I left it outside. She'll find it and she'll get so excited, and she'll open it and she'll be so pleased. (*He eats some more, and thinks of his parcel*) Don't go to sleep, Bun.

Bunny I'm tired.

Oz You've been at home all day, doing nothing.

Bunny It's very tiring, doing nothing. Mary got very tired doing nothing. Just waiting ...

Oz You've got to find things to do, Bunny. Snap out of it. Come on, snap out of it, snap out of it ... (*He goes to Bunny and pulls his arm. He sees the blood*) What's the matter with you? You're bleeding. What've you done? What did you do that for? Bunny, wake up. We've got to do something. What shall we do? Stop it, Bun! Stop bleeding.

Bunny falls over

Don't do that! Here's a towel. It's best not to go to sleep, I think. I don't know. (*He starts to panic. He pushes and pulls Bunny, throws water over him, wraps him, unwraps him until his panic suddenly stops and calm returns*) A good postman should always be prepared. String. Scissors. (*He fetches his "parcel gear" and cuts two pieces of string. He ties a piece round each of Bunny's* wrists) There you are Bun. All neat and tidy, ship-shape and Bristol fashion. For Christ's sake, stop bloody bleeding, Bun. Arms in the air. Come on, hold them up and the blood will stop running out.

He holds Bunny's arms in the air and looks at the phone. He has to drag Bunny along with him in order to keep his arms up and reach the phone. He dials 999

Ambulance please. . . . Oswald Barrington. Fifteen Elm Court. . . . Five nine two five one eight. My friend has had an accident. On the floor. I'm here. I've got his arms up. It's all right, Bunny. I've done very well (*He puts down the phone*)
Bunny I'll have to go back to the hospital.
Oz Yes, you will. The ambulance is coming.
Bunny THE hospital.
Oz No, you won't.
Bunny I want to, Oz.
Oz Why? We're out in the big wide world, you and me. Working men. We've got a telephone.
Bunny Let my arms go, Oz.
Oz No.
Bunny They look after you there.
Oz They closed our bit. You can't go back.
Bunny Untie the string.
Oz No. I went on a postman's first aid course. They do a lot on dog bites. I reckon all dogs should be muzzled.
Bunny You should be muzzled, you talk such crap.
Oz Bee stings and bangs on the head. They do all that . . .
Bunny Let me down, Oz.
Oz You might die.
Bunny I want to die.
Oz But we're friends.
Bunny So let me die.
Oz I'll be on my own. You can't leave me on my own. Everybody does that, and I don't want you to do it.
Bunny You left me . . .
Oz And look what happened!

There is a silence. Oz continues to hold up Bunny's arms, changing his position to make himself comfortable

Bunny!
Bunny What?
Oz I thought you might have gone unconscious.

Bunny No.
Oz I'd have to check your tongue.

Pause

I will get circumcised.
Bunny It doesn't matter.
Oz I will.
Bunny All right.

Pause. Oz remembers his past

Oz I put the letters in the river again.
Bunny Oh, no.
Oz They kept getting mixed up. I looked in my hand and it said number twenty-eight and I put it through the door, and the NEXT house was twenty-eight and so I went back for the letter, but the people weren't in, then I dropped the letters and they got wet, and the last time I did that, someone wrote to the Post Office, and they told me off. So I put them in the back of the bag, and went to do the next road, and I couldn't find it. It was there yesterday, but it wasn't today, and I had all these letters for Warren Road, and it was gone.
Bunny That's what happens, Mr Burkwood. It's a wicked world, people stealing roads.

Oz puts his jacket on and goes to the "desk" as Mr Burkwood

Oz People steal things from my shop, too, you know. You have to have eyes in the back of your head, if you come to work for me.
Bunny I can't come now, Mr Burkwood.
Oz You can start on Monday.
Bunny Thank you Mr Burkwood. But I can't.
Oz Why not?
Bunny I'm a printer, Mr Burkwood.
Oz Well, I'm a postman and I haven't let that stop me.
Bunny No.
Oz Nine o'clock then. You can have my secretary.
Bunny She hasn't got red hair, Mr Burkwood.
Oz I'll keep her then.
Bunny Yes.

Oz rises and extends his hand over the desk

Oz Good. I look forward to seeing you.

Bunny collapses unconscious

Bunny! (*He climbs over the desk desperately trying to revive Bunny and lift up his arms. He starts to chant*)

> Oh please God, please let the ambulance come.
> Oh please God on high
> Don't let Bunny die

       Oh please God on high
       Don't let Bunny die
       Oh please God on high
       Don't let Bunny die …

There is the sound of an ambulance siren gradually becoming apparent over Oz's chant. Silence. There is a banging on the door. Oz starts to cry as he stumbles towards it

CURTAIN

ACT II

Robin's and Julia's flat

The room is very bare. There is one bed with blankets, a table with two chairs on one side of it, and a mirror and a conglomeration of items of make-up. On the other side of the room is a "castle" made of empty Coca Cola tins. There are eight on the first row, seven on the next etc.—thirty-six in all. Next to the bed is an upturned box with a birthday card on it

Robin enters, carrying a plastic shopping bag. She goes to smile at the castle. She takes a cheap box of talcum powder from the bag and transfers it to an original "nice" box on the table. There are clouds of talcum powder. She sits at the table and puffs the powder all over her face

Julia enters. There is something about her clothes that is slightly strange and flowing. She carries her "collecting" bag

Julia I've found some. I've washed them. (*She puts six used Coca Cola tins on the table*)
Robin Six?
Julia Yes.

Robin opens her purse and looks inside

Come on!

Robin gets out three pound coins and puts one each into three tins. Julia waits expectantly

Robin I haven't got any more.
Julia Why not?

There is no reply. Robin powders her face. Julia grabs the purse and looks inside

What have you done with it then? That's what you've done with it.
Robin Somebody gave me that, honestly.
Julia Where? In the street?
Robin It's only talcum powder. See. Smell it. It's horrible, really, but I've run out you see. I put it in the face powder box, because I thought, you can't really tell, and someone didn't want it, and just gave it to me. One of the men downstairs.
Julia You shouldn't talk to the men downstairs.
Robin I didn't.
Julia Not at all?
Robin No.

Julia Didn't you say thank you?

Robin is confused

Robin Does it look all right?

Julia takes the puff and smooths out the powder on Robin's face

Julia What did you do with the money?

Robin points to her bag. Julia takes out six full tins of Coca Cola

They're full.

Robin I didn't think you'd find any. People are silly. They don't just throw them away—they squash them up and throw them away as if that makes it all right. But it's still litter, isn't it? If they didn't squash them first, it would be much better for us.

Julia I always manage to find some.

Robin You sometimes have to go a long way. Sometimes on the bus. You leave me for a long time, Julia.

Julia You shouldn't have bought full ones. It's a waste of money.

Robin So are bus fares. (*She adds the three tins with £1 coins in them to the "castle"*) Will it reach the ceiling do you think? How much do we need to go to France?

Julia I don't know. They haven't got next year's brochures in yet. But it will be over a hundred pounds each. It's not growing fast enough.

Robin No.

Julia You want to go on holiday, don't you?

Robin Yes.

Julia We've got three empty tins.

Robin I'm sorry.

Julia What are you going to do without?

Robin I don't mind really. Whatever you say.

Julia You can do without coffee.

Robin No! I'll get a migraine. I'll get a migraine, Julia.

Julia You won't.

Robin I will. Think of something else.

Julia It's the most expensive thing. We'll make up the missing money sooner.

Robin Just one in the morning. I've got to have that one.

Julia Look, I stopped smoking so that we could build our castle.

Robin It'll hurt. I'll die.

Julia I didn't.

Robin It didn't hurt you.

Julia It did hurt me. I was shaking all over. And sweating. It was like having the flu. I had pain everywhere.

Robin You did have the flu. And I had it.

Julia It was giving up smoking.

Robin I'll take them back.

Julia You haven't given up anything yet. You'll thank me for it in the long run.

Robin No ...
Julia We'll enjoy ourselves much better, if we've both given something up.

Robin applies two thumb knuckles to the pressure points at the back of her neck

Robin I'll have to stay like this for four days. I've done it before you know. My husband said I wouldn't have so many headaches if I gave up coffee. And it takes four days. And four nights. It's a living death. I won't survive this time. I was younger before.
Julia That's what we've all got in common. We were younger before.
Robin I'll have to go to bed.
Julia All right.
Robin No light, no sound.
Julia I'll go out.
Robin What will you do?
Julia Go collecting.
Robin What will I do if the pain comes, and you're out?
Julia You can moan, and I won't hear you. That'll be best for both of us.
Robin I'll die.
Julia Nobody dies of migraine.
Robin I suppose that's something else everybody has in common? Well, I might just be the exception.
Julia You'll hurt yourself if you keep doing that.
Robin It stops IT coming.
Julia Why didn't you stay off it?
Robin What?
Julia Coffee. When you gave it up?
Robin People kept having coffee mornings ... (*She puts more powder on her face*) Would you say I was pretty?
Julia Yes.
Robin I was always pretty. But you get something good like that, and something bad always goes along with it.
Julia You're putting too much on. You mustn't do that.

Robin dusts vigorously. She puts her hand on Julia's arm

Robin Please let me have a coffee.
Julia Don't touch me!
Robin I'm not!
Julia What did you get to eat?
Robin It's time to go to bed.
Julia You didn't get any food!
Robin I couldn't get tins, and change, and food! Go to bed.
Julia It's not time.
Robin Yes it is, it's time.

They get into bed very carefully, one at each end, not touching each other. Robin opens a full tin and takes a drink

I don't feel hungry at all. It fills you up.

Julia pretends to smoke

Julia   I can blow smoke through my nose and make rings. Look.
Robin   What did they tell us to say?
Julia   I ...
Robin   I ...
Julia   Am ...
Robin   Am ...
Julia   In ...
Robin   In ...
Julia   Charge of myself.
Robin   Charge of myself.
Julia   You're touching me!
Robin   It wasn't me. It was ... Tim! (*She pulls out a toy elephant*)
Julia   Slim.
Robin   Yes he is.
Julia   Tim—grim.
Robin   No he's not.
Julia   Tim—prim.
Robin   Tim—dim. Ahh you're not really, Timmy.
Julia   Timmy—Jimmy.
Robin   Two of them. Twins.
Julia   Twins—bins.
Robin   Shins.
Julia   Spins ... wheeh! (*She spins the elephant round the room*)
Robin   Don't! He'll get sick. (*She gets up*)
Julia   Prick.
Robin   Trick.
Julia   Kick, Dick, tick, lick, flick ...

There is a knocking on the door

Robin   Knock ...
Julia   Clock ...
Robin   Frock ...
Julia   Shock ...

They tail off and look at each other

Robin   Who is it?
Julia   I don't know. (*Loudly*) Who is it?
Robin   Shhh. Is it a visitor?
Julia   There aren't any.
Robin   No. It's ... um ... someone.
Julia   It might be.
Robin   Come to take us back? (*She puts her thumb knuckles into her pressure points and starts to moan*)
Julia   Shh. Stop it. Shhh.

The knocks and moans get louder

   Stop!

Silence

Robin Plop! (*She looks up*) Who was it?
Julia I didn't go.
Robin It might have been important. It might have been for me.

There is a long pause, then Julia goes to answer the door. She returns with a parcel

Julia It was the postman's knock.
Robin Yes, Mr Postman.
Julia I've got a parcel for . . . the lady in number seventeen.
Robin That's me. I'm number seventeen. Is it me?
Julia We're both number seventeen.
Robin It's for me.
Julia Who would send you a parcel?
Robin Leighton would.
Julia It's not from Leighton.
Robin You don't know. Where's it from?
Julia Outside the door.
Robin Where was it posted?
Julia London.
Robin Leighton might be in London. Yes, I think he probably is.
Julia No he's not.
Robin Well, do you know anyone in London?
Julia I did. Lots of people. When I lived there.
Robin They've probably all moved by now.
Julia Overspilled. When things spill over, Robin, it makes a mess.
Robin What?
Julia They should have left us where we were. (*She puts the parcel on the box by the card and they sit on the bed*)
Robin He knows where I am. I get a card every year. He knows when my birthday is. I just don't know where he is quite.
Julia I don't know where anybody is now.

Robin picks up the card and reads it

Robin "Happy birthday, darling." My husband used to call me darling. I don't know where he is either.
Julia I never had a husband.
Robin You had a lot of men though.
Julia I can't remember any of them. None of them ever sent me a parcel.
Robin It's for me, then!
Julia No! Because sometimes they said they would, and now maybe one of them has. They didn't put my name on because they forgot it, and that's understandable because I've forgotten theirs.
Robin Do you suppose it could be from one of the . . . one of our . . . not friends . . .
Julia Enemies?
Robin One of the others. From there.

Julia It could be a bomb.
Robin What!
Julia It could be. If it's from there.

They sit and look at it

It was just that a lot of men needed me. There was always somebody who was unhappy. There was a steelworker from Wales, and he couldn't make steel any more because they'd closed the steelworks. Isn't that sad? All your life you're a steelworker, and then you can't make it any more. He came to learn to be a teacher. So that he could go back to Wales and start community projects with other unemployed people. He was sat on the bench outside the post office one day and he was crying. I asked him why. It was the steel.

Robin I don't understand that. They still need steel things, don't they? That new gate they put across the road at the hospital. That was made of steel, wasn't it. And knives and forks and things.
Julia I took him home with me. I can't remember his name.
Robin They all have the same names in Wales, don't they.

Julia reaches out and touches the parcel

Julia It's soft. I don't think it's a bomb.
Robin If we were back there, we could ask someone. It's so difficult to know what to do sometimes.
Julia We've made lots of decisions. We've got the castle and we've got our holiday plans. That's what they said we should do. Make plans. You open it.
Robin I think I'll have my sleep now. I'm tired.
Julia Because it probably is from Leighton.
Robin It's probably from one of your sad people.
Julia I always wanted someone to call me a lady.
Robin Then you open it. Because I think you're a lady. You're nice to me.
Julia Do you think so?
Robin Even when I do silly things.
Julia I do silly things as well.
Robin Everybody does.
Julia Open it.
Robin I'm getting a headache, Julia. I'll have to close my eyes.

She puts the covers over her head. Julia picks up the parcel

What are you doing?
Julia I'm taking the string off.
Robin Is it off?
Julia Yes. Do you want to do a bit?
Robin No. Tell me the next bit.
Julia The paper's sellotaped down. I've got it undone.
Robin Is the paper off yet?
Julia The brown paper is, yes.
Robin What is it?

Julia There's some more paper. Tissue paper. It's something red. (*She takes out a beautiful red dress. She stares at it, puts it down and gets back into bed*) It's for you.

Robin comes out from under the covers, gets out of bed and picks up the dress. She holds the dress against herself as though looking in a mirror

Robin I'd like to try it on please.

The "saleswoman" helps Robin to don the dress

Julia Fits like a glove. Perfect. Exquisite. Oh, madam, what chance brought you into my shop today.

Robin It's my wedding anniversary ...

Julia Well, congratulations. Just by looking at you, I can tell your husband loves you very much.

Robin Can you?

Julia He adores you, would I be right?

Robin He told me to buy a new dress. He's taking me out to dinner tonight.

Julia He'll love this one.

Robin But it's Leighton.

Julia Leighton?

Robin My little boy. He's not very well, you see, and I don't want to leave him. I should be so worried, I shouldn't be able to eat.

Julia Oh dear. Is there no-one who could sit with him?

Robin The baby-sitter, of course. But it's not the same, is it? When you're a little boy and you're ill, you want your mummy, don't you.

Julia What's the matter with him.

Robin I don't know. A virus, the doctor says. He's often ill, you see, and my husband gets cross.

Julia That's a shame.

Robin It seems like I put Leighton before him. I don't, of course. I've got a very good baby-sitter, but it always seems to happen that Leighton is ill, just when my husband has organised something ... and then he blames him, you see, and says that he does it on purpose. (*She starts to take off the dress*)

Julia It's very difficult being a wife and mother. But it'll never look as good on anybody else, madam. He'll like you in it.

Robin He will, yes. He'll say, "Darling, you look beautiful."

Julia Perhaps your little boy will be feeling better by the time you get back. You'll be able to leave him with the baby-sitter and have a wonderful evening. Who's looking after him now?

Robin He's asleep. It's not far. I came in the car. I had to get a dress. You do see, don't you. My neighbour, Mrs Scales, she's looking in for me actually. Yes, I'll have it.

Julia I know you'll be happy in it.

Robin They're supposed to make me happy. My husband and my son.

Julia Shall I wrap it?

Robin I'll wear it home. I'm in the car—it won't get dirty. I haven't got time ... (*She throws her other things into a bag and whirls across the room,* *calling upstairs*) Leighton! Darling, I'm home. Are you awake? Yes? Are you all right? Sweetheart, I've got a new dress. It's beautiful, and it'll make you feel better to look at it. I have to be beautiful for Daddy. It's our wedding birthday today, Leighton. When Mummy and Daddy were married. Daddy wants to take me out tonight for a treat. A party for grown-ups. You don't mind, do you. Lally will come in and look after you . . . Leighton darling, we'll only be gone a little while. Just for a bit. It'll be all right. Please, sweetheart, just this once, don't make a fuss about it. Daddy will take someone else if I don't go with him. Leighton, please, please . . .

Julia has gone back to bed. Robin takes off the dress

Do you want to try it on?
Julia No.
Robin I'm hungry.

Julia looks at her

I get a migraine if I don't eat.

Julia goes to the castle and takes two tins with £1 coins in them and gives them to Robin

Julia Go to the chip shop. The straight way. Just down Warner Road and back. Don't talk to anyone.
Robin I can talk to the chip shop man.
Julia Yes. Ask for one fish and two portions of chips. We'll share the fish.
Robin Yes.
Julia Put your clothes on.

Robin dresses and goes out

Julia picks up the red dress and puts it on

It doesn't matter, you know, that I saw you cry. Because I'm a stranger, and sometimes you can say things to strangers that you can't say to your family or your friends. They sing in Wales, don't they? The men. The miners. Do you know any miners? Yes. It must be wonderful to hear all those voices in harmony. Tell me your name. William Evans. Can you sing? Sing for me. No, don't cry any more. Here. Come here. Lay your head on my breast, Billy Evans. Do you hear it beating? It beats for you. For your heartache. Things make life change, my love, but the beat goes on. Listen. While I hold your head to my breast. Love me, Billy Evans, for then you will feel better. In this strange town, in your strange new life, love me and you will survive. (*She takes off the dress*) When I'm a traveller, I'll come to Wales and look you up . . . whatever your name is.

Robin enters

Robin I was quick. I went straight.
Julia Did you get fish and two chips?
Robin I got more than two, I got loads!

Julia gets two plates from the floor, where most of their domestic stuff is stacked, and puts the food on them

Julia Toads!
Robin Ugh! Who'd eat toads?
Julia You do in France.
Robin You don't.
Julia Well, frogs. Their legs.
Robin Only if you want to. You don't have to.
Julia It would be rude not to.
Robin But we're going to France.
Julia Eat it up.
Robin I feel sick.
Julia You'll get a headache.

Robin puts her knuckles into her pressure points and moans. Julia puts a chip into Robin's mouth

You went and bought them. They're nice.
Robin I don't want to go to France.
Julia We decided.
Robin I want to stay here.
Julia We have to plan ahead.
Robin Why?
Julia Because they told us.
Robin They don't have to do it.
Julia WE want to do it, Robin. We want to be travellers. If we're something, we're somebody who counts. Right? We're saving, so we're savers. And when we've done that, we'll get our tickets and go to France. We'll be travellers.

Robin moans louder

Where are the pills? I'll get you a pill, and you'll feel better. We've forgotten the pills all day today. (*She finds some pills*)
Robin These are yours.
Julia Well, they'll stop you getting depressed, if they don't help your head.

They each take a pill

Robin Can you get me some more?
Julia I do everything.
Robin You know where to go.
Julia You go to the doctor.
Robin You know where he is.
Julia *You* know where he is.
Robin Yes. I'm sorry. I rely on you too much.
Julia Shall I tell you the trouble with you? You never had to do anything for yourself. First your husband, then there, then me.
Robin I want to be independent, Julia. I'm trying to make decisions.
Julia You got all the shopping wrong.
Robin I didn't. I bloody didn't. One fish and lots of chips. (*She holds up the*

plate to show Julia and the food falls off. She beats the floor) I did it right.

Julia puts the food back on the plate and gives it to Robin

Julia You did it nearly right. You'll get better.

Robin remembers when things went wrong

Robin I'll get better, Leighton. Please eat quickly. We're late today. I'll be a
better mother. I bought you a book. It's all about adventures, and it's got
soldiers and princes and a king and a beautiful maiden. Look, she's got a
red dress like Mummy's. Please eat up, sweetheart, because I've got to
clear the things away ... (*She starts to clear up the mess*) ... and get the
washing-up done. It's not fair for Daddy to come home to a mess, and
you've got to have a bath.

*She sits Julia on the edge of the bed and takes off her shoes. She mimes running
a bath etc.*

Little dears must be clean to go to bed. That's part of my job, you see, and
Daddy won't come and kiss you good-night if you're not sweet and fresh
from your bath. Only we have to hurry, please. Leighton, hurry for me—
he'll be here soon, and I want to read to you about the soldiers and the
maiden, and there won't be time, and I won't be a good mother at all ...

*Julia lies on the bed. Robin picks up the book and the elephant and puts them
tidily on the floor. She turns to her imaginary husband*

I'm sorry. I meant to get everything tidied up by the time you came home.
Are you early? No, of course not. I was reading Leighton a story—I got
him a new book. What do you think of it? It's quite a manly book, I
thought. With soldiers ... I'll comb my hair. Do you want a bath? I'll just
have to clean the bathroom—got a bit splashy today. You'll go and kiss
him good-night won't you? Please, kiss him good-night.

Pause. She goes and kisses Julia

There, little dear. That's from Daddy. He's been working so hard today.
He has to put his feet up and have a rest. We haven't got a wardrobe, Ju.

Julia What?

Robin Where shall we put the dress?

Julia I don't know.

Robin Oh. (*She wanders around without solving the problem*) I don't know
where to put it. Don't go to sleep. Help me.

Julia It's all right. It isn't your dress. You don't have to do anything with it.
It's mine. I'll look after it. (*She folds it up and puts it back in the brown
paper, reading the address*) I did it once—for money. You can't be a lady
after that, can you? I did it more than once ... I did it ... for a long time.
It's a disgusting thing to do, isn't it? I'm a disgusting person. (*She hugs the
dress to herself*) It's just a parcel, Mum.

Robin And what's inside? Show me. I don't want any secrets in this house.

Julia It isn't a secret. I was going to show you. (*Julia takes out the dress*)

Robin Whose is it?

Julia It's for the school trip to France.

Robin You're not going on any bloody school trip to France.
Julia My friend, Annie. Her mum didn't want it any more.
Robin I know when you're lying, my girl.
Julia I bought it.
Robin Where did you get the money from?

There is no reply and Robin slaps Julia's face

Answer me.
Julia From my boy-friend.
Robin Boy-friend? What boy-friend?
Julia It's no-one you know.
Robin And why not? What's wrong with him? Oh, I can see what's wrong with him. Throwing his money away on fancy stuff. What does he get in return?
Julia What?
Robin What do you do for him in return, you dirty little madam?
Julia I don't know what you mean.
Robin Oh yes you do. I know men, my girl. They don't give something for nothing. They'll take something for nothing, given half the chance, but they don't give it away.
Julia Well, then, neither do I.
Robin I knew it! You little trollop. Tramp. Whore.
Julia Surely you don't believe that?

Robin shakes the dress at her

Robin Why then?
Julia Because he thinks I'm beautiful. Because he loves me, and he wanted to buy me something beautiful.
Robin Because he wants you on your back with your legs apart!
Julia No!
Robin I won't have men buying your favours, and neither will your father. I could see it in you right from the start. Even as a tiny tot, you would flirt with any man who set foot in this house. You never gave a thought to the worry I had, did you, having to watch your every move in case you got into trouble. It would never surprise me if you came home pregnant one of these days.
Julia Oh, don't worry, Mum. I wouldn't come home.
Robin You'll end up on the streets, that's what you'll do.

Pause

Julia Just once, a long time ago, somebody gave me a dress. I knew it would never happen again. I can't remember his name ... It's taking us so long Robin. I was just thinking. I could do it again. Get money off men. Sometimes I got quite a lot, and you don't really have to do much—just let them put their head on your breast, and tell them they'll feel better.
Robin No, Julia. You can't do that. No! I mean, where would you go? There isn't anywhere. That's our bed. And you'll get diseases, Ju. You got diseases before, you said.

Julia You can go to clinics ...

Robin No, there are worse ones now. I'll go without coffee, and we'll save faster and go to France, only you mustn't go with men again because you'll get ill ...

Julia I will if I want.

Robin They'll touch you!

Silence

Nobody gave me the talcum powder. I stole it. I could do that with other things. Coffee. We won't have to buy it. And bread. Milk. Biscuits. We could save lots. You'll be really busy, collecting.

Julia You'll get caught.

Robin I won't.

Julia You'll get caught, Robin. They'll send you back.

Robin I promise I won't.

Julia They have cameras and television and detectives everywhere.

Pause

Robin Do they know I stole the talcum powder?

Julia Yes.

Robin Oh.

Robin I could ask Leighton for some money. He's doing very well now. When he was a little boy, he used to say he would look after me when he was grown up. He would. I'm sure he would.

Julia You don't know his address.

Robin It's in the card.

Julia He never puts it in the card.

Robin Oh.

Julia You should put it away now. Your birthday was over a month ago.

Robin Just one more day. (*She reads the card*) "With all my love, now and forever, Leighton." Bless him. He always says such nice things.

Julia He always says the same things.

Robin He's amazing. His memory ...

Julia It's always the same card.

Robin He knows how much I love it.

Julia Why doesn't he tell you where he lives.

Robin He forgets.

Julia You've forgotten!

Robin Get into bed. We haven't been to sleep yet.

Pause

They'll be cross with us if we don't have our afternoon nap.

They get into bed

How long have you been here?

Julia I can't remember.

Robin A long time.

Julia Yes.

Robin I'm here for a rest.

Julia Oh?

Robin My husband decided. "Darling," he said, "they tell me you need a rest, and there's a lovely place you can go to where they'll look after you. I'll come and visit you," he said.

Julia I haven't seen him.

Robin Oh, he'll come. I have to settle down first, and I mustn't get upset, and I might if he visits too soon ...

Julia Why do you need a rest?

Robin I don't know. They said ...

Julia You've probably had a breakdown.

Robin (loudly) I haven't!

Julia Shhh.

Robin I haven't broken down. I wouldn't do that. I just ... I don't know.

Julia Would you like to be my friend?

Robin Thank you. Did you have a breakdown?

Julia No.

Robin Oh.

Julia It was men.

Robin Men?

Julia They crawled everywhere. All over my body. And into my head. I couldn't get them out.

Robin What men?

Julia (loudly) I can't remember their names!

Robin Shhh. Shall we go to sleep now?

Julia I can't sleep.

Robin Why not?

Julia In case anybody comes. I don't want them to touch me. God, it's awful. Don't touch me!

Robin No.

Julia I didn't think you would. That's why you can be my friend.

Robin You must go to sleep sometimes.

Julia They gave me sleeping pills.

Robin Didn't they work?

Julia I spat them out. Then they gave me an injection. I screamed. I wouldn't stay still. They tried to hold me down, but they couldn't. Gave up in the end—said I'd fall asleep on my feet. But I never did.

Robin I could watch over you while you sleep. I could. I used to watch Leighton while he slept to make sure nothing happened to him.

Julia And you never fell asleep yourself?

Robin Not while I was watching.

Julia All right then. Just for a minute. I'm so tired. Please don't let anybody crawl on me ...

Julia goes to sleep and after a while, Robin tries very carefully to get out of bed. As she moves, Julia stirs and Robin freezes. Eventually she manages to get out and tucks the covers gently round Julia. She looks at her watch

The Lights change a little. She puts on the dress

Robin There little dear. At last you've gone to sleep. Mummy's here. Mummy's sleeping with you. And Daddy's gone out. To celebrate our anniversary. I showed him the red dress. I put it on and showed him. "Oh darling, I do so want to come out to dinner with you tonight, but Leighton has a virus. Couldn't we postpone it till Saturday? He'll be better by then. I can't leave him. He won't go to sleep without me. I know most husbands forget anniversaries, and I know you've ordered champagne, and I know we can leave the telephone number of the restaurant, but he won't settle. And no, I won't blame you." For what? Oh, Leighton, it's half-past ten. Why did it take you so long to fall asleep? Who is he with? Somebody, you can bet on that. Somebody I don't know because I never meet people, because I can never go out because of you! You don't love me. You can't love me, little dear, or you would understand. It would be better without you really ...

Julia turns over and the pillow is loosened. Robin picks it up and looks at it for a moment. She presses it slowly over Julia's face. Julia screams and leaps up. The Lights change

Julia Get them off! Get them off! (*She is trying to pick things off her*)
Robin Julia, it's all right.
Julia I hate these things. These sodding crawling things.

She is wild and Robin slaps her face. She quietens

Robin You had your nightmares again.
Julia Afternoon mares.
Robin Shares.
Julia Spares.
Robin Cares.
Julia Who cares?
Robin Chairs.
Julia Nobody cares for us. (*She starts to cry*)
Robin I think you should have another pill. (*She gives Julia a pill*) We care for each other. Sometimes it's you and sometimes it's me. You're the best at it.
Julia Am I?
Robin You're always looking after me.
Julia You're wearing my dress.
Robin It's not your dress.
Julia It bloody is. You've stolen it.
Robin I haven't. I wouldn't.
Julia You're a thief. You steal things all the time.
Robin No I don't.

Julia picks up the talcum powder and throws it at Robin

Julia You stole that. You stole my dress.
Robin Stop saying that. It's the lady's dress.
Julia I'm a lady. You said so. I could be.
Robin Who sent it to you?

Julia Someone.
Robin Who?
Julia A man.
Robin Who?
Julia Billy Evans!
Robin Billy Evans! What Billy Evans! You made that up. You never knew their names. You only knew their bodies.
Julia Take it off.
Robin No it's mine. It fits me. It's beautiful. I'm beautiful. It's mine.
Julia Who sent it to you?
Robin Leighton did.
Julia He didn't.
Robin You don't know anything.
Julia Leighton's dead.
Robin You're a fool.
Julia He's been dead for years.
Robin He sends me a card every year. On my birthday.
Julia I send the card every year. The same card. You're the fool. You're the one who doesn't know anything. Look! The same card every year.
Robin Leighton! No! (*The realization dawns slowly*)
Julia He's dead.
Robin No. No.

A moan begins in the depths of her until she screams and cries and runs berserk, wrecking the room. She sinks in silence to the floor

I killed him. I killed my little dear. I thought he remembered my birthday.
Julia He does, darling. I send the card but he remembers.

Julia holds out her arms. Robin backs away

Robin I'm not allowed to touch you.

Julia puts her arms around Robin and they hold each other

He didn't send me the dress.
Julia No.
Robin Then it's yours.
Julia No ...
Robin Somebody nice sent you the dress. You're the lady in number seventeen.
Julia No ...

Robin smooths Julia's arms

Robin There's nothing crawling on you, Ju. You're smooth.
Julia Yes.

They look at the mess

You've made a big hole in our savings. We'll have to start building them up again.

They start to rebuild the castle

Robin My husband used to go to France. I was supposed to go with him. He put me on his passport.
Julia Passport ...
Robin But I couldn't go.
Julia We need passports to go to France.
Robin Haven't you got one?
Julia No.
Robin How do you get them?
Julia I don't know.
Robin If we were back there, we could ask.
Julia I'll ask the doctor.
Robin No. I'll ask the doctor.
Julia Or the post office. You could ask there.
Robin I will.
Julia Or perhaps we'll go to Wales. You don't need passports to go there.
Robin We'll go to France, Julia. And you can wear the red dress.
Julia Next year ...
Robin Yes ...
Julia Perhaps.

CURTAIN

ACT III

The men's flat

It is tidy. Bunny is in bed. He has plasters on his wrists

Oz brings in a tray with a meal on it. He puts it on Bunny's lap and smiles broadly

Oz You're home.

Bunny I don't need to be in bed, Oz.

Oz Rest and relax. The thing is, they let you out.

Bunny Yes.

Oz You didn't believe they would, did you? You were convinced you'd have to go back.

Bunny It's when I've done something, Oz, and it's not me doing it. Like it's another Bunny standing in front and at the sides and all round me, who pretends he's me, and pushes into me from all around, and then I have to do what that other Bunny wants. And it's not me at all. Yet it is. Well, everybody else thinks it is. And then they take me away because they think it's him. But really it's me. And I didn't want to do anything. I didn't want to do this, Oz. (*He indicates his wrists*) He did this.

Oz I know that. I told them that. Not the real you in your right mind would have done it, and it was the real you I came to visit in the hospital, and they could see that, and it was the real you they let out to come home again. We don't want that other Bunny back here, Bunny.

Bunny No.

Oz And guess what?

Bunny What?

Oz produces a parcel

Oz A welcome home present.

Bunny opens the parcel. It is a dictionary

Bunny Oh, Oz. A dictionary.

Oz It's a brand new one with the very latest words in.

Bunny Oh Oz. (*He starts to read it*)

Oz And guess what else?

Bunny Oscitation.

Oz What?

Bunny "Yawning. Inattention. Negligence."

Oz yawns

Oz I'm not inattentive and negligent. I've worked jolly hard to get everything all ship-shape and Bristol fashion for you coming out. That's why I'm yawning because I'm tired.

Bunny I didn't ask you to.

Oz I wanted to. You're my friend. And I made lunch, which you must eat up if you're to get better. And I've done something else. Do you want to know what it is?

Bunny You've got a job.

Oz No. No, I haven't. Shit, Bunny, why did you have to mention that?

Bunny Otiose.

Oz You don't have to read it now, Bun, you've got to eat now.

Bunny "At leisure, lazy, unoccupied. Sterile, futile, not required, serving no useful purpose, functionless . . ."

Oz That's not fair, Bun. I have been doing things. I've organized a party.

Bunny That's me, isn't it? Otiose.

Oz No, it's not . . .

Bunny Unoccupied . . .

Oz You're occupied reading the dictionary and getting better.

Bunny reads again

Don't look at the *O*s any more.

Bunny (*sadly*) It's the nicest present anyone's ever given me. Obituary . . .

Oz Look, I'll find you a nice word. Here you are—scatophagous. Oh, shit.

Bunny What does it mean?

Oz Eat up your lunch——

Bunny takes the dictionary

Bunny "Feeding on dung."

Oz —it's steak and kidney.

Bunny I can't eat it, Oz.

Oz I made it especially.

Bunny I know.

Oz I don't think you have any idea how much effort goes into cooking a meal. You take it all for granted. The time, the expense, the love that goes into it!

Bunny I'm not hungry.

Oz It's protein. I want you to make an effort and eat it up. Have a rest after, and be fit for tonight.

Bunny What's tonight?

Oz I told you.

Bunny can't remember

A party!

Bunny A party of what?

Oz What do you mean, a party of what?

Bunny A party of brain surgeons, tax inspectors, traffic wardens . . . ?

Oz looks at him in amazement

Oz Music, booze, food, women.

Bunny I don't like kidneys.

Oz I like kidneys and I'm the cook.

Bunny Oz, I'm ill in bed. I can't go to a party.

Oz The party's coming here. I've organized it . . .

Bunny And I'll be even iller if I have to eat the kidneys.

Oz grabs the plate and eats everything on it during the course of the following

Oz Music! (*He puts a "Party" tape into an old cassette player*) Booze! (*He produces some cans of lager*) Food! I've done cheese straws and vol-au-vents. With kidneys in! They had a really good offer on kidneys. And tarts. You're going to ask me about the tarts aren't you.

Bunny No.

Oz What sort they are.

Bunny Not prostitutes, Oz.

Oz The tarts! Hah, very good, Bun. Lemon curd prostitutes.

Bunny What are you talking about?

Oz Ask me.

Bunny I don't know what to ask you any more.

Oz I went upstairs, Bun. There was talking behind the door. Knock, knock, knock. Silence. Nobody came. Knock, knock, knock. Nothing. I waited. I was patient, Bun. Then, very slowly, she opened the door. The lady in number seventeen. And she's got a friend, Bun, so I thought of you. "Hallo, I'm Oswald Barrington from the flat downstairs. I would like to lend you a cup of sugar. Or some salt. I'm always running out of salt myself, so I know what it's like" . . . and she agreed.

Bunny To borrow some salt?

Oz To come to our party tonight. At half-past seven. With her friend. I would like first choice, Bun, as I organized it. I did really well, talking to her. Ever so well. You're a good boy—you've eaten it all up. (*He gathers up the tray etc. and tucks Bunny into bed*) Now have a rest and I'll be back soon. I'm going to get some things.

Bunny What things?

Oz Things we'll need for tonight. Things . . .

He takes the tray to the kitchen then returns and goes to the front door

It's most important to rest your wrists—you may need them later.

Oz exits

Bunny lies in bed and wriggles his wrists. He gets out of bed. He wears odd pyjama top and bottoms. He does a press-up. Then another. Then a handstand (even if he falls over). He punches the air. There is a knock on the door

Bunny Yes?

Another knock

Is it you, Oz?

Nothing. Silence. He turns to the "desk"

Mr Burkwood. How unfortunate for you that I was unable to start at your establishment on the appointed day. No doubt you have filled your vacancy. Couldn't fucking wait for me, could you? I slashed my wrists, Mr Burkwood. I went to hospital. Ordinary hospital! Exquisite nurses. Oz came to visit me every day. I shall, of course, continue to apply for various situations, and would certainly hope to do better than the position you offered. (*He wriggles his wrist and ends with a rude finger sign*) And so farewell, and may all your troubles be secretarial ones. (*He sweeps away and opens the door in one movement to find, to his astonishment, that . . .*)

Robin is standing on the other side

Bunny shuts the door, puts his suit jacket on over his pyjamas and slowly opens the door again. They say nothing. He steps back. She remains in the doorway

Robin Are you the man downstairs? That is, downstairs from upstairs?
Bunny No, that's Oz.

Pause

Are you the woman upstairs?
Robin No, that's Julia.
Robin } (*together*) { She's my friend.
Bunny }   { He's my friend.

There is a long pause whilst they absolutely don't know what to do

Bunny Would you like to borrow some sugar?
Robin Yes. All right.

He goes and gets her some in a cup

She remains in the doorway. He hands it to her. They stand

Bunny Would you like more than that?
Robin Yes, all right.

He brings her another cup

They stand

Is your friend out?
Bunny Yes.
Robin My friend's out. She's gone to get things.
Bunny He has.

Robin suddenly comes into the room

Robin I can't come. I'm going to have a migraine. But you just can't not turn up, can you? It's only polite to say if you can't come, and I can't. Julia wants to come. We've started again, you see, and she says we've got to make an effort.
Bunny That's what Oz says.
Robin Does he?

Bunny Yes.
Robin Are you?
Bunny What?
Robin Making an effort?
Bunny I can't, I'm ill.
Robin I am.
Bunny I've been in hospital.
Robin Oh God . . . Oh God . . . hospital. (*She drops the cups of sugar on the floor, and presses her knuckles into her head and moans*)
Bunny It's all right. I'm out now.
Robin *I'm* out now but what does that mean? It still hurts just as much. And I can't find anything. I can't find my husband.
Bunny I can't find my wife.
Robin Why are you repeating everything I say?
Bunny Would you like some more sugar?
Robin No, this is fine.

They get down on hands and knees and push the sugar back into the cups

Bunny Where did you leave him last?
Robin I didn't leave him. He left me. There. I can understand why now. He loved me very much, and I loved him but I did the most terrible thing in the world, and he couldn't love me any more after that. You can't blame him, can you. He was so good to me. He asked them to look after me and to forgive me, but it took a long time. I killed his son, you see, so he had to leave me.

They rise to their feet

I killed Leighton.

She waits for his reaction. There is none

So I can't come to the party.
Bunny I'm not going.
Robin You're copying me again.
Bunny I wasn't going before I met you. I was supposed to go to meet you. Or your friend. Oz has got first choice.
Robin Of what?
Bunny Of you.
Robin He hasn't got first choice of me. I've met you first.
Bunny Have we met then? Good, now I really don't have to go.
Robin I've told you everything about me that's important.
Bunny Why?
Robin Because I don't know anybody else. Only Julia and she knows already. I had to tell someone. Just one person. So that it doesn't slip back inside me again. You won't understand what I'm saying, but it's important for me to say it. I'm sorry.
Bunny Names are important. You haven't told me that.
Robin Robin.
Bunny So you're a bird? (*He laughs*)

Robin What's your name?
Bunny Bunny.
Robin So you're a rabbit. Are you scared?
Bunny Yes.
Robin Not of a bird?
Bunny No.
Robin Of what?
Bunny Living. I tried to stop doing it.

He shows her his wrists. She touches them gently

Robin Are you glad you told someone?
Bunny Yes.
Robin You're copying me again!
Bunny Please don't make me nervous.
Robin I'm not.
Bunny I hate being nervous. Because it . . . I . . . Excuse me.

He goes out of the main door and shuts it

Robin Rabbit! Where are you going? Open the door! Leave go of it. I don't
want to be in here. Let me out. I've got a migraine. (*She moans and sits in
the middle of the room*)

Bunny comes back in

Bunny What's the matter?
Robin My head. I've got to be dark. No light . . . no sound.
Bunny Should you go back upstairs?
Robin Have you got any headache pills?
Bunny Pills?
Robin Oh God. Excuse me. (*Robin moans and crawls under the covers on
Bunny's bed*)

Oz comes through the door

Have you got any pills, Oz.
Oz No. Condoms. (*He goes back to the door*) Come in.

Julia enters with her carrier bag

Bunny, I'd like you to meet the lady in number seventeen. We came up the
stairs together, and she's coming to the party.
Bunny I'm not ready yet.
Julia I haven't come yet.
Oz Bunny's resting in bed.
Julia He's not.
Bunny And getting cups of sugar.
Oz And getting cups of sugar.
Bunny To lend . . . here you are. You can keep them.
Oz Not the cups.
Bunny The sugar.

Julia pours the sugar into her carrier bag and gives the cups back to Bunny

Julia Have you ever been to Wales?
Bunny No.
Oz No.

Julia's skin begins to itch and she rubs it. It is the close proximity of the men

Julia The men sing in Wales.
Oz Oh we can sing.
Bunny Yes, we're men.

They sing—nicely. Julia relaxes. The sugar is coming out through a hole in the carrier. Oz is now stuck for words. He wants Bunny to talk to Julia for him

Would you like another cup of sugar?
Julia No thank you.
Bunny I'll go and get one.
Oz I'll help you.

Bunny and Oz go out to the kitchen

Julia scratches viciously at her arms, then pulls herself together

Oz returns carrying a cup of sugar. He looks around for Bunny, who hasn't followed him in. He hands the cup to Julia

Julia (*scratching again*) I had a disease once. On my skin.
Oz Oh.
Julia Thank you for the sugar, Oswald. Is it Oswald?
Oz You can leave off the waldy bit. Just Oz.
Julia As in the wizard?
Oz Did you see it? My mother took me.
Julia My father took me. My mother was cross.
Oz I bet you've got a beautiful name.
Julia Julia.
Oz Caesar?
Julia If you like.
Oz Julia Caesar. That's wonderful. I'd like you to meet my mother. Will you come to tea?
Julia All right.
Oz Actually, she won't show up.

Pause

Julia Goodbye then.
Oz I'm a postman.
Julia Oh, that's nice.
Oz What are you?
Julia I'm . . . a steelworker. I was. I went to Wales to do it. But they closed it down. And I couldn't do it any more.
Oz I thought that was men's work.
Julia That's all you know then.

Oz Blast furnaces.
Julia They have unisex visors!
Oz They have women postmen too.
Julia There you are then.
Oz I'm all for equality. I bet it was more men than women.
Julia Everything always is. I'm a nurse now. I nurse Robin. She's been in hospital.
Oz Bunny has. It's a responsibility.
Julia Yes it is.
Oz Have you ever been in hospital?
Julia No.
Oz No. I haven't.

Pause

Oz This is my postman's hat.
Julia It suits you.
Oz And I have a parcel for ... the lady in number seventeen.

They stop and look at each other

Julia It was from you.
Oz What?
Julia The parcel.
Oz No it wasn't.
Julia Don't you deliver parcels then?
Oz Yes. Parcels are the best thing in the world.
Julia Who was it for?
Oz It was for you. I saw you on the stairs ...
Julia Not Robin?

Bunny enters with a dustpan and brush

Oz Who's Robin?
Bunny A bird.
Oz What bird?
Bunny In my bed.
Oz You've got a bird in your bed?
Julia Robin's in your bed?

They find her

Oz The party hasn't started yet, Bunny.
Bunny *I'm* not in my bed!
Julia Robin!
Oz Has she got a red breast?
Robin I've got a migraine, Julia.
Julia What do you think you're doing, getting into men's beds. I didn't even know you were out.
Robin I can go out without your permission for Christ's sake.
Julia Not when you've got a migraine. I know what you're like when you've got a migraine. You're not responsible for your own actions. Getting into

men's beds. (*There is an echo from the past*) It would never surprise me if you came home pregnant one of these days.

Oz Is she pregnant, Bunny? I should have done the shopping sooner.

Robin I was pregnant. When I had Leighton, I was.

Bunny She killed him.

Silence

Robin Yes.

Silence

Oz Would anybody like a cup of tea?

Oz exits

Julia is scratching herself

Robin Julia, I'm sorry I was in the man's bed. (*She tries to put her arm round her*)

Julia Don't touch me!

Robin Oh, Ju. (*She sits beside her*)

Bunny I thought I would go to the party after all. Silly me! It's not a pyjama party is it? (*He starts taking off his pyjamas and putting on clean clothes, shirt, suit etc. He combs his hair. By the end of the speech, he is looking presentable*) I went to a party with Mary once. She's my red-headed wife and she was feeling particularly otiose at the time due to the fact that she was just a wife and mother and being awfully neglected by me. I was in a position of some industrial importance at the time, and therefore specifically unotiose. I admit, I neglected her, and I didn't understand her, and she was putting on weight, although I could hardly see how *that* was my fault. And on top of all that, she wanted to go to a party, given by her friend, Hope, who was even fatter than Mary and had six children and her husband made love to her every night. That's what Mary told me. But my head was so full of work problems that I couldn't make love to Mary at all. Which is why she wanted to go to the party, because it was a "Hope Springs Eternal" party, and she thought I would relax and make love to her afterwards. When I was driving home, she kept on about it, and I said I couldn't wait till we got home, so I stopped in a lay-by and told her we'd make love in the back seat. She was really excited, and got out of the car to get in the back seat, and I drove off and left her on the A-three-two-one. I went to bed because I had to get up early for work, but the police knocked on the door. They'd picked Mary up and decided to bring Mary home. I didn't want her home. I couldn't get out of bed because I was cold and my legs wouldn't work, and they broke the door down. Mary's hair wasn't red any more—it was grey, and the policemen were grey, and the world was grey, and I was paralysed . . . (*He breaks down*)

Julia gets up and pulls his head to her breast

Julia It's all right if I see you cry. Lay your head on my breast and you'll feel better.

Robin I met him first. Take him off your breast.
Julia He's crying.
Robin He's not. (*She pushes Bunny away*)
Bunny I am.
Robin Well, stop it. Men don't cry. (*She slaps him*)
Bunny Well, fuck you!

Oz enters

Oz Bunny, there's no sugar.

Robin picks up the cup of sugar and throws it all over him

Robin There's some sugar.

Pause

Julia I don't take sugar in my tea.
Robin I don't.
Bunny I'm not in a sugary mood.
Oz Very well.

Oz goes out

Bunny starts to make a space on the table

Bunny I know what it's like, losing your temper.
Robin Don't understand me.
Julia You've upset her.
Bunny I'm sorry.
Julia Breaking down like that.
Bunny Yes.
Julia What are you going to do about it?
Bunny I don't know.
Robin When Leighton was upset, when he'd fallen off the end of the big
    bookcase because he was trying to reach his daddy's books on Grand Prix
    racing, and he bumped his head and had quite a big bruise, and a twisted
    leg, and he was very upset—I kissed him better.
Bunny Do you want me to do that then?
Robin Do I, Julia?

Julia shrugs slightly. Bunny and Robin can't decide. Then he kisses her

Oz enters with a tray

Bunny rushes to help him

Oz I don't want that one, Bun. She's crazy. You can have her. She's been in
    your bed anyway. I'll have Julia Caesar. She's got superior tits. (*He picks
    up the milk jug*) Do you both take tits?
Bunny Milk.
Oz Milk. Oh shit.
Julia Robin has a tiny bit and I like a bit more.
Oz Hah! Bunny has a tiny bit and I have a bit more!

Bunny Shut up, Oz.

Oz That's circumcision for you! I like a lady who likes a bit more. You sit next to me, Jules. You can sit next to Bunny. And don't hurt him if you don't mind.

Robin I only killed one person you know.

Julia She's got over that now.

Robin I have to keep telling people.

Julia No you don't.

Robin I've got to learn to live with it, Ju.

Julia I'm fed up with living with it.

Oz Would you like to live with me? (*He laughs*) Tart? Oh! left 'em in the kitchen.

Oz exits

Bunny He's good at pastry. He was trying to get a chef's job, then he got busy visiting me in the hospital, and had to give it up till I'm better.

Julia But he's a postman.

Bunny He used to be.

Oz enters with tarts

Julia Aren't you a postman now then?

Oz looks at his watch

Oz Oh no, not now. Too late in the day. Early mornings, I'm a postman.

Bunny A private postman.

Oz Trained by the Post Office, mind.

Bunny But now he posts private things.

Julia Who for?

Oz Private people.

Bunny It's like buses. They've gone private.

Robin It's like us. We've gone private. We used to be public property.

Oz Like prostitutes.

Julia No! Not like prostitutes! (*She gets up and crosses the room away from them*)

Oz Oh shit. Oh shit, oh shit, oh shit. (*He gets up and paces the room away from Julia*) I hate Ford Granadas! They're the cause of all the trouble in this world.

Bunny They are.

Robin They are.

Bunny Chlorofluorocarbons in the exhaust fumes ... holes everywhere, getting bigger by the hour ...

Robin It isn't prostitutes, Ju, it's Ford Granadas that cause all the trouble in the world. Julia hates prostitutes.

Bunny I do.

Julia I hate men!

Robin Men and prostitutes ...

Oz I like prostitutes!

They all look at him

They don't want to go home and meet your mother, and they don't want you to talk to them, and they don't mind if you're fat and ugly, and if you haven't been circumcised. They don't care about drips!

Julia turns to him

Julia Can I try one of your tarts?
Oz Oh. Yes. Lemon curd, bilberry jam, or ginger and rhubarb?
Julia I'd like to try one of each.
Oz Oh shit.

They go and eat tarts

Bunny If you like, you could tell me lots of times instead of telling lots of people.
Robin Thank you. Do you have a son?
Bunny Mary has. She's got one of each. She says . . . she told me . . . after I left her on the A-three-two-one . . . (*He stops*)
Robin What are they called.
Bunny Michael. And Martha. They don't look like me.
Robin Leighton didn't look like me.
Bunny Didn't he?
Robin He had my husband's little nose. Really little noses they had. And funny ears. With kind of nobbles on.
Bunny They've got red hair, like Mary.
Robin What did she tell you?
Bunny That they weren't mine. She says I never had it in me.
Oz It's her you have to have it in.
Robin She probably only said that because you left her on the A-three-two-one.
Bunny I don't know. It's something you can never be sure of, isn't it. Whether you've fathered your children? A woman knows—she gives birth and she knows. But the father could be anyone.
Robin Not if she loved you.
Bunny She didn't! She wanted to eat me. Like that spider.
Robin Poor rabbit.
Bunny I don't see them now because I don't know.
Robin How sad . . .
Julia (*to Oz*) They're awfully good.
Bunny At least they're not dead.
Julia The tarts?
Robin They're called Michael and Martha.
Julia The tarts?
Oz Did you know Julia Caesar was a steel worker?
Julia Ashley, actually.
Oz What?
Bunny They hadn't invented it, had they?
Robin Thank you, Rabbit.
Bunny What for?
Oz What?

Robin For saying "dead". It's very good for me. Say it again.
Bunny Dead.
Oz What hadn't they invented?
Bunny Steel. Romans didn't have steel.
Robin He is dead.
Oz Not the Romans. Julia Caesar.
Julia Ashley——
Bunny He was a Roman.
Julia —actually.
Oz Ashley?
Julia Not Caesar.
Robin He is dead.
Bunny He's a dead Roman.
Oz He's a woman.
Bunny Julius Caesar?
Oz You're an incredibly attractive woman.
Julia Thank you.

Oz nudges Bunny

Oz Do you like cheese straws and vol-au-vents?
Julia Yes.
Oz With kidneys in?
Julia I love kidneys.
Oz Do you? Do you! (*He nudges Bunny again*)
Robin They wanted Leighton's kidneys.
Oz For vol-au-vents?
Robin For somebody else. For another little boy whose mother hadn't killed him. But my husband said no. I said yes. But he said no. So they didn't.
Oz I tell you what Romans did have.
Bunny What?
Oz Orgies.
Julia Do you want an orgy then?
Oz No. Oh no. I'm just saying, that's what they had. And straight roads.
Julia That have no turning. They went straight from heaven to hell. But they were lucky. At least they had a taste of heaven.
Oz Why don't we start the orgy now? Party. (*He puts on the tape and starts dancing*) Would you like to dance?

Julia picks up the carrier bag and goes out

Julia! Julia!

Oz runs after her

Robin starts to dance, in her own world. She drifts round Bunny, touching him. He gets nervous

Oz comes back

Bunny Mr Burkwood, your secretary is dancing on the sugar.

Oz She shut the door in my face. That's big tits for you. I'm going to make a cake.

He goes to the kitchen

Robin wants Bunny to dance

Robin I remember this tune. I used to dance with my husband.
Bunny Let's do something else.
Robin I think we ought to have a little brother or sister for Leighton, don't you?
Bunny Leighton's dead.
Robin All the more reason, don't you see.
Bunny No Robin. I . . .
Robin Call me "Darling". Dance with me.
Bunny Robin.
Robin "Darling."
Bunny Darling . . .
Robin Dance with me.

They begin to dance

It's wrong for him to be an only child. I was an only child and it was very lonely. I was lonely all my life till I met you.
Bunny I'm not me. That's the trouble. I'm someone else.
Robin Who?
Bunny I don't know. There's another me. He does things I don't want him to do.
Robin You could never do things I don't want to do.
Bunny I could. I did. And I do.
Robin Pretend you're my husband. Pretend you're him. Tell me you love me, darling.
Bunny No.
Robin And I'll be Mary.
Bunny No.
Robin Tell me. You promised you'd tell me every day. And every night . . .
Bunny I tried to, but there wasn't time.
Robin There's time now.
Bunny I have to go to work.
Robin No, you don't.
Bunny I do, Mary. I do. You know I do . . .
Robin No you don't, you don't you don't . . .
Bunny No.
Robin It's time for me now.
Bunny Yes.
Robin I love you . . .
Bunny I love you . . .

They hold each other

Oz enters

Oz Bunny, there's no sugar.

Julia enters in the red dress. She has a small parcel

They look at her. The music continues to play

Robin Julia.
Julia He meant it for me.
Oz You look like my mother.
Julia You wanted to give it to me?
Oz Yes.

She holds out the parcel

Julia It's for you.
Oz Oh shit! For me!

He opens it. It is a packet of sugar. He is overcome

Oz Oh shit! You're a really kind ... lady.
Julia I always wanted ...
Oz OH SHIT! (*He turns up the volume of the music and starts to dance in front of Julia*) We'll start the party now, Bun.
Bunny It's not half-past seven.
Oz Never mind. Nobody ever got sacked for being early!

All four disco dance together, laughing and enjoying themselves. Oz splits the four cans of lager and gives them one each. They open them and drink whilst dancing. This happiness and music build to a climax as they dance into two couples again. Oz holds out his hand to Julia, and she takes it, but her horror of being touched by men gradually comes upon her as Oz becomes more salacious. At the same time, Robin moves in on Bunny

Oz You're beautiful, Julia Caesar.
Robin We'll be a happy family and walk in the woods and have a dog. And you can invite your work people home for dinner ...
Bunny I can't bring my work people home. I haven't got any work.
Robin You'll have to get a job.

Oz pushes Julia towards the bed and presses his mouth down on hers. She protests and struggles

Julia Leave me alone ...
Bunny I can't. I've got you.
Robin And the new baby.
Bunny I'll get tired and I'll ache.
Robin You'll have to look after us, you know. We're your responsibility.
Bunny I have to be at the factory.
Robin When you come home darling ...
Bunny Stop it, Mary, go away ...
Robin I love you. Talk to me. Hold me! Make love to me!

Julia struggles against Oz

Julia I'm a lady!
Oz I need you.
Robin Make love to me.
Bunny No!
Oz Yes.
Julia No!
Robin Yes!

The couples grapple with each other as the music finishes on some discordant note. They stop. In the silence of an ended tape, Robin presses her knuckles into her head, and sits on the floor, moaning. Bunny crawls into his bed and thumps his wrists together in rhythm. Julia takes off the red dress and lets it fall to the floor. She scratches her arms. Oz sits at the table and starts to eat

Oz You're right, Bunny. The party doesn't start till half-past seven.

CURTAIN

FURNITURE AND PROPERTY LIST

ACT I

On stage: 2 beds with bedding. *On Bunny's:* dressing-gown, clothes. *On Oz's:* clothes, postman's hat

Chest of drawers. *In drawers:* clothes. *On top:* shaving foam, razor, razor blades, bowl of water, towel

Table. *On it:* telephone, dishes, Bunny's references, letter, c.v., can of hair lacquer, comb

Chairs. *On one:* ironing

Ironing board. *On it:* suit, iron (plugged in)

Newspaper

Umbrella

Parcel-making kit—tissue paper, brown paper, sellotape, scissors, string, pen, stamps, stamping kit

Suitcase containing clothes, white tissue paper, carefully folded dresses including a red one, mail bag

Off stage: Pie and tart **(Oz)**

Personal: **Bunny:** blood sacs on wrists

ACT II

On stage: Bed with blankets, pillows, toy elephant

Upturned box. *On it:* birthday card

Table. *On it:* mirror, make-up items, face powder box with puff, bottles of pills, book

2 chairs

Castle of empty Coca Cola tins (36)

Plates, cutlery, other kitchen equipment stacked on floor

Off stage: Plastic shopping bag containing cheap box of talcum powder, 6 full cans of Coca Cola **(Robin)**

Carrier bag containing 6 used Coca Cola tins **(Julia)**

Parcel containing red dress **(Julia)**

Fish and chips **(Robin)**

Personal: **Robin:** wrist-watch

ACT II

On stage: As Act I

Strike: Tray, food, plates, cutlery, etc.

Re-set: Tidy room
            Bunny's suit jacket and clothes on chair

Set: Parcel containing dictionary under bed
            Cassette player, tape
            Cans of lager

Off stage: Tray with plate of food, cutlery **(Oz)**
            Cup of sugar **(Bunny)**
            Another cup of sugar **(Bunny)**
            Carrier bag with hole in it **(Julia)**
            Cup of sugar **(Oz)**
            Dustpan and brush **(Oz)**
            Tray with cups of tea, jug of milk **(Oz)**
            Plate of tarts **(Oz)**
            Small parcel containing packet of sugar **(Julia)**

Personal: **Bunny:** plasters on wrists
            Oz: wrist-watch

LIGHTING PLOT

Property fittings required: nil

2 interiors. 2 flats

ACT I Day

To open: General interior lighting

No cues

ACT II Day

To open: General interior lighting

Cue 1	**Robin** looks at her watch *Change lights a little*	(Page 29)
Cue 2	**Julia** screams and leaps up *Return to previous lighting*	(Page 30)

ACT III Late afternoon

To open: General interior lighting

No cues

EFFECTS PLOT

ACT I

Cue 1   As **Oz** chants   (Page 16)
Ambulance siren, gradually increasing, then stopping; pause then banging on door

ACT II

Cue 2   **Julia:** "... tick, lick, flick ..."   (Page 20)
Knocking on door

Cue 3   **Julia:** "Shh. Stop it. Shhh."   (Page 20)
Knocking becomes louder

Cue 4   **Julia:** "Stop!"   (Page 21)
Knocking stops

ACT III

Cue 5   **Oz** puts on tape   (Page 45)
Party music

Cue 6   **Oz** turns up volume of music   (Page 47)
Increase volume of party music

Cue 7   Couples grapple with each other   (Page 48)
Music finishes on discordant note

MADE AND PRINTED IN GREAT BRITAIN BY
LATIMER TREND & COMPANY LTD PLYMOUTH

MADE IN ENGLAND